The Container

to Kim!

Nessa McClosy

Note To The Reader

I am a poetry therapy practitioner / certified poetry therapist, which has offered to me an amazing magical carpet ride as a career. What is poetry therapy, you might ask? Here is a bit of a description, from an article I wrote in 2001.

"Our current, hyper-speed society has brought about much isolation. We seek connection with others to gain vital nourishment and offset the soul hunger that results from isolation. This is one reason for the increased use of the arts in therapy. The arts have a unique ability to connect us to each other and to our world. Music, drama, art, play, and poetry provide creative pathways that comfort at the same time that they guide through physical, emotional, and/ or spiritual pain and healing. Poetry therapy (also known as therapeutic writing, bibliotherapy, journal therapy) works in a creatively healing process by providing a structure for feelings or experiences and a connection with another person(s), the poet, and (if in therapeutic session) with others as well."

Metaphor is naturally found in poetry. The metaphor of this book, *The Container*, came to me when I took a workshop with a Native American to forge a bowl out of a sheet of copper (cover photo). Later, when I began training as a poetry therapist, I realized that the piece of paper is another container, for emotions and ideas, for rants and praise. This book is the result of years of my using paper and pen as container. That is also the work that I do for individuals and groups, facilitating others in creative containment and self-empowerment.

To learn more about poetry therapy, see my Facebook group, Wildridge Healing Expressions, or the website www.iapoetry.org.

CONTENTS

≈ © ≈

Mothering

Living

Healing

Creating

Musing

Coping

CONTENTS

When used for healing, the Container (whether paper, bowl, garden, or universe) is metaphor for holding what seems unholdable.

These words, phrases, lines have been holding my world together so that I can look at it and make meaning out of the days, weeks, months that keep going by, faster and faster.

May you find connection/community and perhaps something to take away for yourself in these poems.

Dedications

This book is dedicated to my great aunt Pat LaBelle, who believed in me and had long been encouraging these poems into print.

I also wish to thank Christopher Dostal, Brad Miller, Elsie McCasey, and Gene & Lila Weisberger, who were or still are wondrous inspirations and supports for my writing life.

The Container

Mothering

Longing and Belonging

longing
always I am
reaching into my soul
for the place to stand firmly
grounded

heart blast
as solar chimes
resound while I write this
savoring aloneness and peace
in tears

holding
sorrow and joy
in my hands at one time
longing is deep and belonging
is sky –

sky looks
upon me now
I breathe slowly
and feel held by the world as if
mothered

Keeping Too Much in Fear of Losing Something

Why don't I have his first word at hand?
I don't remember it;
digging to retrieve it
is archaeology.
This is more valuable than gold.

Day by day, I sort and file
stack after stack,
box after box,
room after room,
and it comes down to a foggy life.
The question begs: Why?

I become an archaeologist
carefully searching through dust and dirt,
not knowing what will be unearthed until
one piece emerges that leads to another
until, after all, a structural life is assembled.
Not the real life, but one that could be true.

My eyes don't see past
the fog of living,
and still I dig,
believing my heart knows what is true
and it will beat thus, to let me know
when both the word and I are found.

Singing Myself, My Son Forward...

Birds sing and people complain.
When people sing, birds must be amazed.
Listening to others sing, whether birds or people,
I get lost in time in reverie.

On the coldest of nights one winter,
I transported myself to a past summer
sitting in a farmer's field
listening to various blues artists.

The notes of a trumpet riff are
similar to my own long harangue
of the troubles facing my son
as others only stare at his problems.

Why don't they sing to him
a lullaby, in any language,
even if he cannot understand?
What if we could sing children well?

I make up a new song myself,
remembering past times of joy
hoping to take him into a better future,
a song that can be there for him,
even when I am not.

Porch Light

It is 4:25 a.m.
The neighbor has a light on
over her front porch.
Maybe she's up now
making a birthday cake
for the man next door
whose wife had to do
two things at one time
and so she offered
to help out —
now each woman will
do one thing at a time.
This act of kindness
fashions a solid footing
in my abraded foundation
of overwhelming stress:
the world's hurts and callousness,
my country's identity turned
upside down like one of those drawings
where the once smiling face
becomes a devilish scowl.
And the stress above all,
as my son struggles with anxiety
(and psychosis or perseverative thought),
my own dreams craze my nights.
An early morning thought of sanity
is this: it might be as simple
as keeping our front porch lights on.

A Meditation on Curves and Corners

He walks gingerly, with limping steps,
scrapes on the tops of his feet
and elbows and knees,
after falling from his bike –
curves and corners
the biggest problem.
Three or four times
in fewer days,
he has encountered the earth
intimately, brutally.

Still, he doesn't like to hear
that he should wear shoes while riding.
He bristles and quickly walks away from me.
After a moment, I realize
how he is becoming his own,
stubborn self, all 16 years of him;
I am in good space,
in harmony with the world.

My heart has been scraped
through collisions with experience.
It remains open and tender.
Yet challenges are always there.
The curves and corners
require negotiation.
Not knowing what is ahead,
trusting in grace.

Appeal for Naught

Gray day,
I steadily do paperwork
on the computer.
When insurance appeal person
returns my call I yammer instead of cry;
she reports
that Occupational Therapy
services are denied
by the state – diagnosis
not severe enough.

    What is the diagnosis?
    What is severe enough?
    He's lost a year of school; I've lost my son for a year.
    Who will help me get him back?

Earlier, I watched a hawk
sitting in the tree,
being blown slightly
in the wind.
I notice his ragged feathers
before he takes off, soaring up until
I cannot see him anymore.

The sky is gray today.
The wind blows a lone oak leaf
slowly down, spiraling, to the ground.
The hawk might find a mouse on his search today.
Now I start to cry all my tears.

Writing In the Deep Quiet

Pacing like his grandfather
the links there entice me
to wonder again. But later,
wonder must wait, as he tells me
he's hearing voices in his head
and I worry about what his teacher said,
"We don't want to lose him."
Fear paralyzes my internal organs
and digestion stops somewhere
along the middle of my colon.

It seems that the strains of the world
have come to bear on this household.
War rages on the news: genocide and murder.
Alzheimer's increased its toll on seniors
(taking down the grandfather of this boy-man
with autism spectrum disorder). The boy-man
mostly disappeared before my eyes, replaced
with mania, obsessions, disconnectedness. At 3 a.m.,
finally, a deep quiet envelops the house.

While solutions are difficult –
if possible at all –
I spend the night sleeping next to him,
my arm draped across his chest
in fierce certainty
that there's no way in this world
that I will let him go lost.

Beyond

Some day
far into the future,
I hope I will have the wherewithal
to gather notes and calendars
and odd poetic tries
together into a timeline
of this frustration.
This poem is a beginning.

It has been a lifetime
 — my son's —
and some past years
have felt more like double
their actual length.
Is my sense of urgency
too quiet for most special ed teachers?

It could be that school professionals
tasked with mothers
have shrouded ear muffs
so that they only see the mouth moving.
They reply with a nod of their heads
or to offer a promise
that will never be fulfilled;
a momentary truce. They aren't
long-term thinkers and often break their word.
Some kind of thrill-seeking junkies they are,
hearing gratitude for their compassion.
Then they dust off any residue
before going back to their own sweet lives.

Another school year draws to a close;
the teacher wonders
if I want a certificate of completion
for the [lack of] education my son has
accomplished (or the lack of teaching
that has been accomplished).
Misunderstood and given up on
by teacher after teacher, all just
keep plodding onward
no matter how many
fall behind.

You might think the teacher would
have the decency to flinch
at the look of shock on my face as I searched
for some meaningful answer to his question.
I think he gave up on me, as well.
Have I left the planet; am I on the moon now?
Or have I skipped on past, on past even Mars
landing on Jupiter.

CT Scan Results

Nothing abnormal showed.
Talking with the doctor
just now
(he called).
After I hung up,
I stood still.
It felt
like
falling
into
darkness,
into mystery.

Holding it all in my hands.
Feeling it all in my heart.
Writing it all into
the book of my tears.

Following the Bouncing Ball

Central High School, Forest Hills School District
Autism Program with Mr. Thomas
Mrs. Secor, Social Worker

Then Kent Education Center,
Kent Intermediate School District
Autism Classroom with Mr. Joynt
Mr. Eavens, Social Worker
FHSD OT Ms. Thompson

Then Emotionally Impaired Classroom with Mr. Luke
Ms. Copeland, Social Worker
KISD OT Ms. Schuitema
Inappropriate placement, says Mr.Luke

Then Goodwill Industries, in Grandville
(noisy, dusty, busy environment)

Then Methodist Church Community Center,
Grand Rapids
(quiet, safe, secure environment where everyone
looks asleep, including the teachers)

And then. finally:
CTEC Vocational Assessment -- Rejected student
CBOT Vocational Assessment -- Rerouted back to KEC
(Rule out less restrictive environment?)

This is for the time period from January to
December 2005, concerning the logistical placement
politics for the bouncing ball named Christopher,
one mother's very huggable son.

Living

Breathing

Somehow it seems an answer,
repotting the spider plant and
taking down the hanging leafy plant,
tearing away all the overgrown trails.
Having cleared all that,
an electrical cord shows
where the plant used to hang,
but I later cover it with
a string of silk flowers.
And then, finally,
vacuuming.

Life's abundance can be overwhelming,
but there's clarity in the open window.
— dead leaves gone now —
I see a deep breath
of fresh, clean air.

The Gift in Vacuuming

After the newness of carpet stopped smelling
I plugged in the vacuum to gather the stray pieces of yarn.
The sucking hose ran back and forth across the floor,
and carpet strands jumped in front of my eyes,
playing hopscotch while the sun
fell in stripes at a lovely slant.
Natural and man-made remnants of joy
led onto visions of days to come,
adding a dining room table
purchased from a dear friend,
and searching for varied chairs
to add to the mixture.
Joy is multifaceted for me,
and can begin in the mundane task of housekeeping.
There in my mind are both past and future gatherings of
friends and family for conversation and warm companionship.
Our first meal was and forever has been Thanksgiving.

Tired

Some mornings I am just too tired to live.
Bones and muscles ache;
some can't be found even with stretching.
Ahhhhhhhh. This is the best time
for me to surrender to the Spirit of Life.
So odd, this happens when I feel at one with the ants,
the wind, the dead beloveds, and the ill.
I linger in these moments when I reckon
with my soul the value of my life.
It's not like me to do the math (all those pesky details),
so why do I worry so much with it all?
So tired of everything in this crazy life,
I lay it all down for this moment of reverie
and just be gnarly, bumpy me.

The real trick, I suppose,
is of juggling the doing
and being of this existence.
Whether you are poet, preacher,
soldier or leader of a country,
whether you are the banker or the farmer
or the real estate developer,
whether you are a mother or a father,
a child or an elder:
what is the reverie that stops you in your tracks
or humbles you to cry at the moth's lot in life?
Or will you go to all the buzzing of electronics
in your ear and your own voice carrying out
what you have to do today?
Coming back to my own gnarly meditation,
hoping that tomorrow, I will remember
perspective, wise perspective.

The Air, Just Before Rain

Once again today,
the sky is ready to pour down
its sustenance.
Yesterday, I took note
of the fullness of air
as I drove along
the long road to a
meeting that wouldn't be.
A young woman
pedaled her bike,
probably mindful of the coming rain
yet resolutely pedaling.

I drove on into the city
where no one would join me.
I lingered even
in a room of comfortable sofas
and soft lighting.
As if I were a desert,
I soak up the sustenance
that mingles in the air
before it finally rains.

Terrible Inheritance

The sun rose today
just like
any other day
But then
my heart sank
I was
sad.

It was as simple as
the doctor asking
if there were any blood diseases
in my family history.
Like leukemia,
she said.
My dad has leukemia,
I stammered,
my eyes wide.
His mother died from
what we know now was lupus.

A terrible inheritance…

My journey is made up of
steps along the way:
this is one of those steps.

Swimming

Yes, I'm breathing right now.
In out. In out. In. Out.
Warming my back makes me
realize the value of the sun,
the hard work of others,
and even my own initiative
to create a better life.

What can I do to best live? Perhaps it is
simply to be. Not to be smart,
beautiful, rich, or anything
other than exactly who I am
right at this minute,
a sincere woman trying to keep on.

Instead of preparing to hibernate,
I keep on keeping appointments
and trying to hold my head above water,
as I never learned to swim well at all.

Sunset, Late Fall

The first real chill today
wind serious about itself
and I donned hat and gloves
    for my walk.

It's my new habit, 2 days old
and just barely in time
before winter changes the shore
    into a different planet.

Tonight, the sun sets softly -
my eyes drawn to the view
even as early nightlife begins
    and nearby tables fill.

I was early to be seated, to capture moments.
Unshared, I hold them jealously.
I co-opt some conversation from the corner,
    leaning slightly into their lives
    in my writerly way.

Walkers with dog on leash
stir birds who linger on the brick walls
as the sky shade darkens, pinks to reds to maroon to brown.
    Another fall day richly ends. Moist and full, my heart.

Resolute Life

Just as the sun opened onto the morning,
my neighbor and I walked carefully
down our icy driveway slopes,
meeting in the middle of the cul-de-sac,
and headed down the street veering
left and right around ice patches.
Each step became firmer, even on some ice
when I missed seeing it,
until by the time we returned home,
the sun itself more assured now,
I was resolute in my steps.
Now to action in this day
with further inspiration from
the quote I placed on the front door
to be seen as I faced
out into the world:

> Look well,
> therefore to
> this day,
> for it is life,
> the very life of life.[1]

MIDLIFE

Mysterious journey to an
Island along the pathway of life's waters
Dawdling between naivete and wisdom
Living both at the same time
Innocently traveling to the next destination
Fond as we are of the present
Exuberant about all the futures.

I Am Sleeping Bear Dunes

i am sleeping bear dunes [2]
lying between the big lake
and the rest of the state.
my hair flies wild in the winds
    when i run up and down
the hills at night
and thunder roars
       across the sky
while i'm stamping my feet.

shifting i am changing
changing i am shifting
markings for travelers
become my building blocks
that i simply move at will

willful i am sturdy
living on for centuries
always elegant
always alone
except for the moon
who visits each night.
we meet always
at a different place
even if ever so slightly,
ever so fleetingly.

from a broad brushstroke
i am the orange ink
arching across a calm beige background.
i am the vellum paper
lying atop a raging landscape
of violence, commerce, and neglect.

i am body hurtling through space
unknowing and knowing of all things.
i am body of stone.
i am body of mass.
i am body of nerves.
i am body of blood.
i am body of frailty.
i am body of trust
in my heart in my body
i am trust of strength of my legs;
walking on
walking on
even darkness
walking on.
i am sure of the light now.
i am body of me.

i am sleeping bear dunes,
centuries past and centuries present,
perhaps centuries future
as winds continue to shift
all of my cells.

My Howl

I.   I heard lies about compassion, fidelity, kindness,
        and all the virtues,
     where they were important and to be strived for, and yet,
     where so often they went against human nature even as babies
     were born into a world
        less than kind to them,
     where, instead, reality was changing as were definitions of
        those important things.
     Love undefinable
        so unquantifiable
           so sweetly devastating in its manipulations,
     Compassion nothing less than what we rarely do for another –
     the golden rule treating each other as one would also be treated.
        Fidelity merely time spent being constant and the days
        that go by beat up one's ken for deliberate choices.
     And kindness, well, that is just too much to expect
     in anyone's busy state of mind and their important work to do.

II. God help me, I still believe in the truth!
              If only I stop expecting so much,
        If only I cry enough to mourn the loss, each one of them,
           If only I just believe in taking one step and another one.
              Yes, I think I did that and still do.

III. And still it is worth it –
even disappointment and loss and heartache and tears
and never getting ahead or secure or knowing
the belief of future and risking failure again and again
and then getting up to try again.
Because even when I cry, it is good;
as the hot wetness is mine,
the stinging burn is mine,
the breath is mine, and
being alive this moment is mine!

Meditation

Swans flying, circling the lake.
After they pass, no ripples,
even the wind is quiet.

Everything is as it should be
in our natural world.
After the swans leave,
I trust in the circle's promise;
they will return next spring.

I circle back around
inside myself.
What silence, peace
on the lake, in my soul.

Dreaming

Dreaming of a cozy world
where safety of everyone is paramount.
Where people are who they are
and can be who they are.
Where understanding might
come over an uncomfortable
discussion
but happens because
the conversants
are courageous
enough to make
no mountain too high
to climb up.
And one will climb up
even when the other lags
always looking back
over the shoulder
encouraging engagement
and movement
forward again.
I dream a lot
making my dreams come true
because I believe in them
and their value in this world
turned colder than
so many hoped it would be.

About Wildness

It is here,
in my roar
best heard in my rage.
My wildness is best felt from
a distance, best left to echo wildly
across a windy plains field.

Beyond Darkness

Out of my darkness [3]
it feels I'll never arrive.
The time of transition
continues and continues
as if I never can change
from who I was and always am
into who I am becoming
and never may be.
Am I simply myself and
always the same?
And yet never the me
that I see as myself.

My eyes are blind seeing
myself as others must see me
and yet I cannot see myself
as I am or do I and deny
the others the truth of
what they see?
Shall I die one day,
remaining unfinished?
Will my life be only questions
and never answers?
Rilke said to live the questions
and my life is a continual stream.

If the dawn never rises
will I still throw myself into the day --
trusting that I do live into each action
though my tongue never knows
that I swallow this life whole.

Calming Myself

I live a simple life, with odd joys,
such as letting the cat stand
on my outstretched legs
as I read a small book of poems
in bed in the early morning.
He wants his food bowl filled.
His eyes implore and then
he jumps off the bed, for emphasis.

    I lay pen or pencil to paper
    and allow assonance and alliteration,
    rhythm and intonation
    to be the music I sing.
    We are astonishing,
    humans with our hearts throbbing,
    intending to live forever
    and yet knowing it cannot be.

It is *this* moment that matters
as the cat returns, purring
and letting me pet him.
His fur beneath my fingers
a sacred assonance,
another poem.

The Blessing of Knowing
a Neighbor

Two birds stop and notice,
Passing is a sacred moment in one's life
whether you are the one who is gone,
or whether you are the one who is going.
The paper boy rollerblades quickly
hopping up the steps to the screen door,
still open for so many in and out.
processing the event as their jobs require.
He is young, perhaps 11, and quick,
and soon darts away again,
after wedging the day's news
in the sliding door handle.
probably unaware, as the young are
if they're lucky.

West Michigan Removal Service arrives in
a gray van, backing in to the driveway.
It's a good thing, a sign of our compassion,
that the body is cared for with reverence,
even if their sign glares someone's ignorance.
Undertakers used to be men,
but these are women, in skirted suits no less,
and they left behind a white rose
on the pillow where
his head was last laid to rest.
Yet he didn't die in bed; he had just returned
from lunch out and feeding the birds.
How to live life, he taught,
even on the day he died.
I'm happy I knew my neighbor.
He didn't die in bed.

Burnt Toast

My greatest blessing is the love
around my heart and soul,
finding warmth in a cold world
learning how to nourish that flame
through long winters
of transformation.
I know that my travels long,
step-by-step, seemingly uphill,
got a great boost into high speed
when a certain most fragile heart
started loving me. When a sturdy
Pegasus took flight and let me
jump on board. And yes,
most indicative of all,
that this certain man
will eat all the burnt toast.

A New Song

How did I finally see their love
as part of the chosen path
that is all of the tense
and weighted down
way that I live in the world?
It was when I heard them say,
under their breath and
when I had my back turned,
"You are never perfect enough.
We love you, but we prefer you
to be perfect."

How I tried, years of good school grades,
job, marriage, and baby,
being the good mother,
carrying half the weight
of a breaking union,
quiet corporate duty
and bearing of disillusionment
until a place in my heart
heard poems that seemed to offer
a rope that I could use to climb
upward and out of a deep hole.
Climbing is my life's work.

As long as the sun shines
up ahead of me,
I keep on climbing,
writing new songs
that I can't quite sing yet.
Here, let me hum a little,
and find a melody.

Healing

Lingering Longer

Her life was really a transparency.
She was born and grew up in an age of speed
towards the future, the unknown.
Who knew? Though the soothsayers named
this as normal energy shift,
her body wasn't equipped to thrive
without pause, without time to herself,
time to nap and rise with joy,
time to notice the swan family and
how quickly their season went by: one week
the young, newly white swan learned to fly,
careening around the lake perimeter.
The next week he was gone and the parents
might have been lonely, but they still looked serene
paddling around the lake together for a time
before they, too, headed south for the winter.

Now, as she looked over her own life,
old memories were fading and
sometimes no longer seemed real.
The pages in her mind were made
of tissue paper, which required a light touch
to turn the pages without tearing them.
She decided she would not cause them duress
instead lingering longer on each page
before she turned to the next.

Writing the Story

It seems that talking isn't enough.
I leave therapy sessions drained but
later don't remember what we talked about
or what insights I gained while I was there.

Well, maybe I remember
but it's not on the
tip of my tongue.

Instead it leaks
out of the end
of my pen
remaining solid
(paper covers rock)
evidence of
this path
seeking truth,
finding the center.

Chop Suey

She met me at the restaurant,
her regular haunt,
which made me think of
the attempted multicultural,
middle-class American dinners
we had at home when I was a child.
Now, I relish those same bland dinners,
realizing how the family
had changed in so many ways,
all of us grown and
some of us dead.

But she insisted and so we sat,
me unsure of what to order
since no other meal could be
that safe blandness of years ago.
Instead, we spoke of her life now,
and I responded kindly,
hoping she didn't notice
that I was a bit distracted.

What We Need

What we need
is wide-enough eyes
to see beyond ourselves
into pain across the world
and know that we are never alone.

What we need
is others having those eyes
to understand our pain,
and hearts with compassion
to help someone.

What we need
is an understanding
that helping each other
will make this world
so much better, our own heaven.

What we need
is to know ourselves as
needing each other
and reaching out
for even a simple hug.

I want to reach out to
the daily scenes on TV news
of despair, destruction, destitution,
and pull those crying into my arms
long enough to know they are not alone.
I send my heart energy instead,
hoping beyond my logical mind
that it will make a difference,

that our world will become warmer
in spirit; I stand tall in the
middle of my living room, expectant,
giving and receiving love
creating this generous world.

The Way

Gentle music flows in a forward motion, guiding energy
into a brand new day, a day where it all is new again,
a day that becomes my birth day, again. I am new,
I struggle to know myself as I change from what was
night to now is day, from a short seasonal year of
autumn – winter – autumn – winter – for the last decade,
or was it my whole life? The owl sitting on the branch
above my head breathes, "Who Who are you?
You… You are becoming you."

So much to put down here, the past so that it is concrete,
and then a sturdy foundation to continue on from. I must
learn the way to live in more balance, like the waves on a

lake with a gentle breeze   ～～

not stagnant on a deathly still day   ——

not raging as when storm winds wildly rock the waves   Ｍ^Ｍ

The hardest thing is to let go and live in myself, not from
outside myself looking on everything and directing
adjustments – a little more smile, a little less, oops,
not the right moment to spill your guts, stop being so
serious... I follow this string of thoughts along, to see
what's on the other end, holding it, keeping it taut.
I move slowly along the string as my guide, learning
to trust all that is within me, for it is me, my life, my own.

Saving The World

Will it save the world
if we let our broken selves pour forth healing:
healing the soil – and our hearts –
with our blood and tears?

Spring follows the dark winter
in the north country.
As the world turns to its own healing
from centuries of humans overwhelming it,
we can honor it by doing the same.

Then, peace to all readers
as we grieve our issues, and
heal one and all, inch by inch,
tear by tear, word by word,
day into new day.

May it be so.

Meditation on a Dark Day

The clouds loom
and my heart seems
to take them into my soul.
Why? I wonder how it is
that denseness of the air
pervades my spirit,
loneliness,
while I wait for something
to happen in this world
that will lighten my soul.

War on so many landscapes
has deadened the human spirit of our today's.
Children, women, men die daily —-
at terrible cost to those who remain.
What are our nights like? Filled with darkness,
dreams of black winds and darker villains?

Today the clouds darken
the sky around me.
I let my spirit rest
in the quiet of this day.
Wandering among words
and the light that I find there,
another day blends
into those before. Yet,
Peace holds onto me tightly.
Lean back, it says,
I'll bear your weight.

Lost

Standing still,
I hear my heartbeat
in the wind blowing by my ear.
Reasoning out my life's path
is not working,
so instead I breathe.
Losing myself in this rhythm –
in and out, in and out,
slowly and slower –
is a new kind of salvation.
Wandering trail after trail
and seeing nothing there but dust,
I could give up and declare myself lost.
Yet, it is an inner prodding
that I listen to: move toward the light.

Answers that I wasn't aware of seeking
come as a river flows downhill,
as a bird takes flight for a new feeding ground,
as young and old alike know that they still breathe.

Divine Healing with Poets

I'm Learning to Love Myself
And all the places inside
that have been neglected
or stuffed down where
they can't be seen –
this is a process of divine healing.
There are no doctors
with medicine strong enough
and there are no men
with arms that are brave enough
and there are no mothers
with chicken soup stocked enough
and after long long long days passing;
there is no patience inside me anymore
and no more desire to ignore these places.

Instead, I have found poets –
friends and journeyers of the dark paths –
those who are willing to let
darkness be
darkness and
alienation be
alienation
and sorrow be
sorrow and
ugliness be
ugliness.
For there is a glimmer of light
within each word of truth
and a new sun rising on each (re)birth.

These ugly, rejected parts of myself,
are like a wrinkled newborn,
long soaking in the dark moist
sustenance of mother-fluid.

Now exposed, clumsily,
are long buried feelings
of shame, rejection,
and all other small feelings
still clinging to survival.
Each word glimmer displays
the possibility inherent in birth;
to live a light-filled life,
shining our true spirits
as beacons.

Cracking Through the Cosmos

He suddenly, surprisingly
leaned into the older, steady man
entering into a hug
that then was offered
in response to the gesture,
gratefully even.
Witness to this exchange,
I felt the tremor,
foundational,
as the man's 3-ton iceberg
of frozen tears mixed
with the dross of his life and
minutely shifted.
Small purple violas sprouted.
I know I saw Paradise
in the middle of the kitchen.

Heart

Again and again
Hardship wrestles with my heart—
Bless the muscle's strength.

The Container

I know this bowl;
my hands formed it from a sheet of copper
firing it 5 times in orange/red-hot fire
pounding it with a large, round stone
while it sat on a cut stump
and I sat on another.

Symmetry was in its making and
Symmetry is in its being now.

It is copper-red with spots of black
where the copper burned in those flames.
As the metal heated, it became malleable
and opened itself to a new shape,
a new use in the world,
becoming a container.

Purpose was in its making and
Purpose is in its being now.

Horsehair is bound with copper wire
strewn with beads: green, red, blue, and black,
and two bone disks mated with clear white beads –
symbols for earth, fire, sky, and more.

Symbol was in its making and
Symbolic it becomes for me.

I placed it on a low shelf in my home
and found I had created an altar.
The bowl appears empty and yet
it has become a powerful container
for it holds my wishes, dreams, and memories.
It can also hold my pain and my happiness,
my loves and my losses, my fear, and my courage.

A similar bowl
in the pit of my soul,
reverberates
as I hold my hand-made copper bowl.
This is how I hear music.

Creating

Elton John

I would like to borrow your
eyeglasses,
even just a few pair.
You see, I need
to look through
some glitzy,
bejeweled,
audaciously fun
specs
for I'm needing
to change
my vision
of my self and my world.
My heart yearns to dare
to try to fly
fast, sure and higher
than maybe I should.
Do you have any
glasses that would
work for that?

Trying to Understand

Her name –
I can't remember her name.
But her face – I see it.

Her face as she folded clothes
from the given pile, into clothes
she might wear, clothes for another.
She folded expertly, with confidence.

Julie had told her to "talk" to me
and so she started telling me
her story. Her face was thin, long,
and she said that she had had
a cleft palate, which had been operated on.
Her family background was full of abuse
and it is remarkable that she lives now,
on her own yet with support,
in a housing shelter for those who would
likely die if left out on their own.
She had been abused by men all her life,
even as a child, by her stepfather,
and her mother called her useless.
How did she survive?

Now she carries two Bibles down the street,
carrying the Word as if it were a talisman
made just for her.
Who am I before this story?
Who am I after knowing her?
I am her human companion for a day.
Ah, the mere survival of humanity.
Write it out, write it out
so that we can remember this one.

Who am I?

Today I am a wanderer within my own life,
lost in possibilities.
I wonder who I really am,
beneath the trappings of what
looks like a person in our world today.
All my emotions:
impatience, melancholy, regret,
yearning, and a tension of action unspent,
these are a thick soup,
capable of sustaining me
for weeks at a time.

Still, others would judge me,
and perhaps rightly so.
For a day spent lost in possibility
remains empty of any of those possibilities.
It isn't so different than any day
of my childhood,
as I read the fantastic worlds
created by various authors.

Yet now, happy turn of events,
I find that life can be encapsulated
in as few as several lines.
Today I am a poet.

How Poetry Comes to Me

On a whisper from far away;
if I don't listen closely
it is just another breeze
on a hot day.

Clear winter day
sound of waves
    solitary life

Winter 1986
San Francisco

Kambare no shiosai shōgai kodoku nari
寒晴れの潮騒生涯孤独なり

Temple Dusk
by Mitsu Suzuki

149

Empty sky
midwinter twilight
    hawk ascending

Winter 1987
San Francisco

Nani mo naki kambo ni tobi no takami yuku
何もなき寒暮に鳶の高みゆく

150

Treehouse

Wildridge house
poetry house
poet's hideout house
sharing with cats
and men
and family
and friends
(and the natural world
so often not invited in:
bugs, a bat once, and mice
that the cats corner).

Nurturing place
that needs work
to nurture me more
so I keep working on it
hoping that wildridge house
remains a
poetry house
poet's hideout house
built for sharing.

Endless Questions

How does smoke curl around the air
curling around the chimney and
why is it so elegant in its curves?

What draws eyes to sunsets
forcing color into lives and
       will memories last forever?

What heals a deep wound - can it
heal itself by loving again and
       how long will it still have to hurt?

What lingers in hearts that makes
lingering life-giving after all and
where does all the incredible hope come from?

Poetry Makes My Day

Not knowing where I am going
is often the best way for me to travel.
Though common wisdom has been
to know where one wants to go
before setting out,
it works for me to start walking,
one foot in front of the other, and
then let miracles happen. Rainbows appear
at the end of a rainstorm. Smiles come my
way even when I don't deserve them. There's
a happy design in the clouds in the sky.
A parking spot opens up just when I need one.
And a poem comes out of the atmosphere.
Into my fingers. Onto the page.
Even without lines on the page, still,
a poem. You might think I was similar to
the wonderful poets who find poems
on their daily walks into nature.

The best wisdom may be that
we are all wonderful poets,
if we just let each poem have its time.
So go ahead, put one foot in front of the other,
start walking, and let another miracle happen.
To you. And to the world.

Open The Door

Go on, open the door that you have ignored for so long,
expecting that it would only be a trick or lead to an empty room.
Without trusting the world, nothing will result
and the room of treasures will remain empty all your life
and you will be bereft.

Go on, trust this world with its doors everywhere.
Open one after the other and remain committed
to trying another even if you find one is a dud.

Here, this one is waiting just for you. Your best
friend is there on the other side. It's your own heart,
beating for your creative spirit, giving it a try. Now
just do that again. Again. Again.

A Rainy, Sunny Day

At first, it's cloudy and quite lovely,
then it rains and that's enjoyable.
I walk with my son and we both get soggy,
and don't mind that at all.
Then the sun pops out,
shining into the living room.
Suddenly I wonder if it had rained at all
and I'm glad that I got wet
as proof for myself
that indeed it had.

What else matters in this world of ours?
Money is too shiny and those grabbing it
hold it tightly in their fists
until blood drips through their grip.
Only after I gasp at the insensitivity
and then meet someone who
has learned this too
can I gather my face into the smile
of such a sunny day again.

I hope tomorrow will be the same.
So often it's not,
and yet I must keep hoping.
Writing, hoping, and then, who knows?
Out into this world, I creep.
Thank goodness for all my calluses.

My Own Yellow Brick Road

The people I love
have expanded my life
in ways mysteriously
wonderful.
How would I have known,
as I watched years ago,
about a Yellow Brick Road
and the search for the Wizard
that my life would be the same.
All who I met
and have grown to love
have become so much more
than He who I was expected to revere
when I knew it was more like a story.
Now I know, the grantor
of my wishes is myself!
Oh! The riches I have gained
on every step of this journey
by opening my heart
to each person along the path.
Long live the Wizard/Goddess!

Shrinky Dinks?

There's a fight within me about the inside world,
and the outside world and how much of each
should remain where it is.
I find so many people who write interesting books
and I want to gulp their wisdom into my mind.
I meet interesting people who I yearn to know
more closely, allowing myself that pleasure
and learning because there's just so much to learn
in this world and it is not within me.
Close in proximity, lie the greatest
learning opportunities:
my partner, my son,
my family, my friends.
And I cannot ever forget
and often do,
and must remind myself
otherwise
that even more valuable
is my own true heart
connected to my brain already full of learnings
specific to my experiences and my soul,
which has its own agenda
for what I shall cherish,
and how I will expand into a world
so intent upon shrinking
the individual.

Musing

Does Loving Do Us Any Good?

Tenderness is in the hands. - Carolyn Forché [4]

Tenderness is in the hands.
Knowledge in the soul.
Turning left or right
has no meaning –
destination never being the point
only what has passed under your feet
and the view you've chosen to look upon.

Even the friends you love and cherish
become but dearest memory
in the changing light.
Marking days by moon spot and
dirt or blood under your nails
leaves you little to ponder
or regret.

And when you touch her face
you can't feel shadows drawn by lowered light
on fragile skin.
You hear her heartbeat
like a train rumbling miles away
passing through town
late at night
completely unknown
by those who sleep soundly.

Seeing What I Hear

An oddly warm November
and though the leaves
have been falling for at least
5 weeks now, I hear them
falling again this morning.

I close my eyes and
really listen to the world
around me, finding that I
am able to "see" colors.
How magical the mind
and body are in collaboration.

The world is simply wonderful today,
hope inspired again by the act
of breathing in and out
and darkening a particular circle
on a presidential ballot.

If only we could really see
how powerful we are...

Vision

Entering on the path
into the wooded darkness
beyond what I can see
and have known.
Or have I?
Something familiar
is in the breeze
and draws me in;
the closer I get
the stronger it pulls.
Cells under my skin
are suddenly alert as if they can see;
they quiver with recognition.

Another Day, Today

Sun shines brightly and
the mind clouds over.
It's not uncommon yet
we are all so afraid of it
that we won't look at those afflicted
in case it might be catching.
Somehow through our masquerading
we become more vulnerable than we
might have intended.
It's so easy,
to move across
that invisible line into
Things Are Not All Right Anymore.

One day you have a job,
insurance, a cat, a home;
your kids are in bed at night
when they should be.
The next day something changes.
It could be anything – a diagnosis
from a doctor advising chemo or
a sudden layoff, well not so out of the blue;
I wonder what nightmare *you* imagine.

Today, the sun comes out.
I breathe in and out.
I can count on one more breath.
And then another.
If I had lung cancer,
I would not take
my breath for granted.

I stop right now
to remember this blessing.
After all, it is
about balance.
Relying on the fact of today,
with or without sun,
such a beautiful day.

My God Metaphor...

Having given up on the pearly gates
and Him who sits on a big chair
with flowing robes
and white hair, beard,
now I choose to see God
in every movement on this earth,
using this name: Spirit of Life.
SOL is in a child's smile,
an old man's broken-toothed whistle,
the cranky bus driver who
snarls, especially at teenagers with
their tattered clothes
boarding his bus with music in their ears.
Everything good and bad has SOL within
and I cannot distinguish anyone
or anything as not SOL.
From today until I die,
I shall be seeing more of
the Spirit of Life
in things that even now
I do not understand.

Walking Through...

...Monkey mind is the guardian at the gate. — Natalie Goldberg

At the gate,
I wonder what my future is,
how the landscape will look
far into the distance.

Fear holds onto the keys and jangles them.
Monkey mind opens and then slams
the gate, repeatedly;
its wooden slats shudder
but it remains solid when I put my hand upon it.

Silence finally, and monkey mind slows in shock.
Fear stands back one or two steps,
as if to clear the way,
and I walk through, onto a sunlit path.

The Light / The Dark

vulnerable and securely fastened
day and night continue.
dead weight
with soul inside and outside
always wanting to fly or
walk slowly through the shadowy woods
even knowing that darkness can also
breed life yet wonderlusting for the
sun rays slanting and reverberating
off the leaves on a lucky tree.
does the tree feel kissed?
as my face does
and i lean into the tree
to hear its heart
never wanting to leave that spot
in the woods
sooner trip over a
                    knotty root
even tho i did know
it had to be there
but it was darkness
everywhere then
and i couldn't see.
i must hold onto a treeeee,
so solid
so sooo open at the top
reaching for the   s k y l y   reaching
even yet sturdy rootedness
into the dark of rich underearth.
i am both afraid
and verrry brave
and so will always forevermorely
celebratilly
look into the dark
and then beyond,
to find the light.

Wooded Prairie Field, October

The world is still out there –
traffic echoes in the distance.
Yet I sink down among the grasses,
ferns, and wild flowers,
beside a small semi-circle of white pine.
The smell of nature's change engulfs my nose.
As I quiet my own breathing,
I hear the Towhee,
and even the gentlest of rustling
as the night wind breathes tonight.
The waxing moon grows larger
each passing day.
Nights are cooling.
As leaves slough from their trees and plants die
their edges brown further inward
seeking the center,
where lifeblood oozes slowly.
Fall, so beautiful in a show of
red, orange, and yellow colors,
is also colored brown
also crackles in brittleness –
the circle of life is dying.
Soon winter will bury the field.
The ground will reach up for its nourishment.
The field lives on even in its dying.

Snow, December 8

8:27 a.m. Saturday morning.
And it happened. Late this year, and
it's a silly childish dream to imagine
no snow at all in Michigan.
Working at the computer, starting fresh,
and then I stretch and turn around.
My eyes stop at the kitchen window and
then swing to the larger living room window,
and yes, from both of these windows,
one serving as confirmation for the other,
it is snowing, big flakes, just like it is supposed
to in December in the north.

It is December 8 and
this is the first snow of the year.
The minister had preached
about evidence of greenhouse effect,
affecting our seasons, our water level.
Rhetorically asked: When will we take note?

It is my own musing that caught me off guard.
Could it be possible that it wouldn't snow before Christmas?
The child within squeaked no, that wouldn't be right!
The adult in me, who drives all over the region, relaxes at
the thought: dry roads are safer.
This morning, it was a spiritual jolt,
that turn of the head view.

I sigh, and relish the fat fluffy flakes deep in my soul, where
memory combines with universality and divine connection.
What will be will be, whether it's what I want or not,
whether it's easy or not, whether I notice or not.

Buddha Cats

I wax philosophical,
maybe because of the rain.
Or because it is fall acting a little
like summer.
Maybe it is because
I'm always hurrying
to get to tomorrow
and then trying to slow my life down.

Maybe it's because I walk after the cats
trying to coax them into my affections
but all I have to say to them is always
the same — you're a good boy — while
I pet their long backs over and over again.
Do they run away from me because they
are tired of this? Or is it instead
an ongoing spiritual lesson about letting
everything come to me on *its* time?

That's hardly what the world teaches,
as I let the animals run wild in my head.

I come back to my breathing, a sigh,
and that funny way of my being in this world:
fully sad at my humanness and vulnerability,
and at the same time
completely in awe of this wonder of my life.
All in one moment of insight
before I go back to my daily life.

So today I'll wait and let a cat (or not)
come to curl on my lap while I type.

A Friend Suggested: Breathe Comma Pray

Breathe comma pray.
Breathe comma relax.
Breathe comma love.
Breathe comma dream.
Breathe comma smile.
Breathe comma laugh.
Breathe comma sing.
Breathe comma dance.
Breathe comma create.
Breathe comma fly.
Breathe comma shine.
Breathe comma dream.
Breathe comma love.
Breathe comma relax.
Breathe comma pray.

Gentle Ripples

gentle ripples surrounding

half-sunken rowboat –

peace maintained within

Decay and Beauty

No matter how many times
someone considers me beautiful,
I know that I am decaying every day
and so my own beauty doesn't impress me.
Instead, I long for a display in the sky – sun, moon, clouds.
Leaves that have decayed for years
have left an amazing floor outside my house.
I walk there knowing that my footprints
matter less than an oak leaf.
My footprint will be fully erased with one rain.
The oak leaf lasts for years and then offers
another form of itself to continue even further.
How I hope that my spirit will land on some tree
where I will hear the wind and see the sun
long after my body becomes earth again.

Flourishing

Why fight the inevitable?
I lean against the very life I lead
in opposition to where it has taken me
for months, years, and all because I
have judged the lines in the soft sand
under the water. The ebb and flow of
the life essence of water is similar to
the constancy of the sunrise/sunset.
The water is inside me and outside of me.
Why not learn to swim with the tide instead
of always against it? Afraid that it will take me
further out to sea? Ah, I fight against my own life
and now, at 50 years of it, at last I see
that the water is more powerful than I
ever can be. It will have its way. Instead,
I must learn to flourish here, just here, inside
my own body, my own fluid community.

Summer Break

summer break –

cool morning breeze

follows dark cloud burst

Navigation

The center slips again.
Directional bias of mine
is away, surfacing above trouble.

Courage seems to be about staying
rather than the adventurous travel of youth
so young and still wise then, too.

Life is piled upon itself now:
mourning my past and
healing from it at the same time.

It's a swampy land,
this collection of unburied feelings
and of course, monsters breed here.

Raising my head, always,
looking for the sun or the moon
if only to find my own direction.

Without the sky, how does one navigate?
Lighting a candle while I shower,
I breathe and pretend it's the sun.

My heart aches for warmth
for comfort of earth-made shelter
molded by hands with care.

It evades me and I walk on,
modern traveler, accustomed to ease
yet understanding it all buries my soul.

The center slips again.
Directional bias is simply – onward.

Instructions

Open your heart again and again. It will be punctured by
sharp rocks and clumsy people, thus you can
rain all your love down on the world.

Welcome challenges. They will wear away your skin,
and you will become shiny and more tender. While you will
sometimes wince, you should also know that you will shimmer
in the sunlight (even when there's just a small ray coming
through a cloudy sky) and your receptivity to hugs will increase.

Find god in all people. Even those who are hard to understand.
Love those people the most, for they will teach you the most, too.

Don't be afraid of anyone. Especially yourself. Live into your skin
and love yourself the best of all. Start glowing from the inside out.

Do it today. Let me see you glowing
when I pass you on the sidewalk.
I'm looking forward to today's journey;
wherever I go, I look for people who glow.

Seed of Gratitude

Begin with silent gratitude. Notice how it feels;
Maybe it feels like a warm shower washing over
your insides. Feel it so deeply that it begins to come
out of your pores, and then has your face softening,
and lips curling up at the ends. Feel it so strongly
that you cannot help but give it voice as song your
whole body joins, singing.

Say to yourself; I am grateful for life, from the
inside out.

Call To Adventure

A good life is one hero journey after another. - Joseph Campbell

When my son was diagnosed with schizophrenia, due to having psychosis, I couldn't quite believe it. I spent many long nights on Google reading listservs until finally, I myself noticed that he got psychotic symptoms whenever he had corn chips. So I stopped giving him corn chips. And then I went further into foods made with corn such as high fructose corn syrup and sometimes citric acid. Finally, the psychiatrist accepted my view and stopped his medication, which also had corn ingredients. That previous diagnosis has now been noted as mistaken in his record.

This is now how I am trying to cope with my own diagnosis of Parkinson's Disease. What if the doctor does not really know what I have but handed me the diagnosis?

How many people are diagnosed without tests that prove the diagnosis?

Initiation to Adventure
The hero must
overcome the obstacle.
The dark wood —
inward journey to birth.

What the hero goes to get:
The end result: the Sun.

Where is my dragon?
Is he stronger than I realized?
What resources do I need?
What if I don't slay my dragon?

The Initiation: Slaying the Dragon
The dragon is inside of me: it may be myself.
Why have I accepted that the journey
will just work out when it has taken

> MY energy to accomplish it again and again?
> If I first slay my accepted dragon
> will I be able to be truly born again?

Struggle is happening inside of me now.
I will need to be very brave to him them off.
My hero's journey of initiation may have parts 1, 2, and even 3.
I must follow the path that appears...

The Return
The hero comes home, changed.
Master of two worlds;
Inner and outer worlds.

Write about the naysayers.
Write about acceptance.
Write about the magic.

The Return: The Things of Magic
Golden opportunity.
Escaping the ordinary life.
The unexpected.
The deep mystery of my own self:
my gut as it were.
Being my best self for myself
and for the world too.

Technically
So perhaps I won't ever slay the dragon...
Instead I have accepted my normalcy, but yet...
It is highly charged with a a magical notion of hope!
So I tend to calm, slowing myself down.

But at the same time, don't ever think that I have given up.
Rather, I believe in flowing, mostly over and around obstacles.

To Change the World a Bit

(After Alice Walker's poem of the same title)

To change the world a bit more each day,
you must cease to be afraid of death.

Why is this so?
Isn't everybody afraid of their own demise?

Certainly I am, especially at the hands of those
more interested in money than people!

And yet I dream a world where
all humans will be free, and able.

Joy, like a pearl
surrounded by darkness,
made into revelry.

To Change What We Can

I am one person but I am one Person!
I can change myself.
I can wait through some pain, at times,
when I think I cannot bear it, I can still do just that!

We are very remarkable bodies, each of us.
Name one thing unremarkable about your body and
I will tell you something new about that for you to think on!
Isn't that ideal!

For Mary Oliver

Your poem,
The Journey,
Started me down the path
Of healing power of poems
And of course,
The healing power of poets.

Therefore you will live on forevermore...

I need only to go outside and spend time with bees or grasshoppers
or grasses, even, and your marvelous lines will come to me,
unbidden, as if you were writing and saying them for the first time
beside me in my own yard!

Holy holy words you wrote. That may be why you are considered
by me as holy yourself. And aren't all those who write holy,
anyway?

Untitled, Meditation

The birds have been chirping rather incessantly this spring, or at least that's what my mind received their songs as. I didn't have the chance to get bird seed this spring so I was assuming they were simply hungry. Like my husband often is, as he eats my food.

But it is good to eat when hungry, I suppose...

When we prepare our grocery list, he refuses anything I offer him for the list, corn chips, or gluten-free English muffins, which I can no longer eat as now I have a corn intolerance. But he could still eat both of these and more. He feels bad when I get upset in the moment when I realize that I cannot eat the fresh guacamole with corn chips. I behaved badly, and now I still pay penance for that.

So I take a big, deep long breath in and out. Let go of that old moment and even the current one of despair of not feeding the birds. Making fried potatoes on the stove top is what I can do in this moment.

Tall Pine Tree

Pussy willow bush grown as tall and large,
wispy leaves with lights,
rose light,
sheep's woolen sweater,
blue flowers,
and oak trees offering huge limbs.

The campy rose light,
used to be in my mother's
guest room, the room with a single bed
and sewing machine.
I hope to plant some rose bushes.
They may not grow,
But then again, they might like
my sunny front yard, with all the garlic,
raspberry bushes, green beans,
and perhaps tomatoes too!

Who would have guessed that I could grow raspberries?
Not my mother, for sure. But maybe she is hanging
around my yard occasionally,
even nodding in approval.
I hope so, anyway.

In the Early Morning Hours

When no one else is up yet,
and the silence is gently quiet,

I hear my heartbeat best.
It is my own motor.

The outdoors of course has already
taken to its workday.
The birdsong lulls me back to sleep,
against my will, leaving the silence alone.

Later in the day, if I try real hard
I can get to that momentary silence again,
when there is no sound in the house.
These are golden moments.

Talking and other ways of being human are fine,
but they are never golden.

Why would I expect that, anyway?

Rising Narcissism

A major bummer
as the news networks
are obsessed with
the agony of schism,
a caricatured juggernaut.
Lack of light or peace
leaves participatory politics
at the side of the road.
And then, like a screeching
needle across an old LP record,
I require escape from
the world, despite my
struggle for belonging –
as I soak up forest gratitude,
sunny balm and surrender
to rebirth – unraveling
every grief experienced.
Self-aware of passion for
mystery, my own voice unknown,
yet grounded in the luck of
endeavor: becoming.

Cloud Pantoum

My friend, you're so far away,
it seems I can't yell loud enough
to reach the distance
even if the landscape is flat.

It seems I can't yell loud enough
to hear myself.
Even if the landscape is flat
you continue to look to the clouds.

To hear myself
I have to chuckle in pain and delight.
You continue to look to the clouds
forgetting the ground you stand on.

I have to chuckle in pain and delight.
I love your eyes.
Forgetting the ground you stand on
I grab the clouds in my own fist.

I love your eyes.
You remember so much there.
I grab the clouds in my own fist!
My friend, you're so far away!

Coping

Lament and Hope

Who made me?
What were they thinking about then?
What were their burdens in life?
How quickly did their daily suns turn?
What did they pass on to me
to bear in mystery
long long into my life
unconscious of any
such belongingness?

Ohhh,
perhaps it's the darkness
of our confused world today ---
full of conflict
of fighting fights
that can't fully integrate
into any psyche.
Such a curtain does
that secret place maintain
for even a small
jewel to remain.
Instead of fighting
we could take out
our shovels
and start digging
for each our own
internal treasure.

Excerpt From An Undated Poem

…dancing with tired feet
connected to a heavy heart
many stones on my path
leave gouges in my skin

I jump, albeit lightly
into my own future
it's too much, I want to curl up
and sleep….

I lay down in the woods
and I sleep
and I dream
of dancing [5]

Writing About Happiness
or Truth
or...

My Orders To Me

Ok. My illness had given me a new purpose:
Write yes just write down as much as possible...

My life is on fire! That is how I feel much of the time now!
Yes, oh to write how I see the world now is remarkable.
It may well be informed by illness, but it is also fueled by
my brain, now thoroughly poetry-soaked,
and pumped up with my inner turmoils about
the way humans live on this great big blue-green ball.

Yes, my time is well-spent on such matters.
Perhaps I may write something that will last, as well,
beyond what my eyes can see.

Abecedarian Poem

A number of reasons why. By the way, it is my health. Covered by the damned doctor as a true failure to connect with her patient. Doctor-be-damned if she didn't care to listen. Even worse, she wanted to protect her reputation rather than her patient's life. For sure, that was not going to happen! Googling was so easy to do. However far I had to go, I was going to find the best doctor I could! Intellectual fodder for anyone to do the same. Just do it, google it: what have you got to lose! Keep going and get it done. Living is my only task now. Maybe I will even find a new cure! New cure is my just dessert. Organic oranges — for health!! Pepperoni pizza is back in my diet now, but I have to make it homemade so it will be organic. Questions about diet comprehending food as medicine. Rascals of the kitchen unite and keep learning! Stop beating yourself into the ground or the grave. There is only one way out of this world, after all! Under this one big sky, we can grow and live more honestly with each other. Valuable good food is important now that we live with so many pesticides everywhere. Which reminds me to promote the local food coop here in GR! Xerox copy of the 60's nearly! Yet and again... Zero sum game, but alive.

I Would Like to Live Like...

a horse, jumping over anything in my way.
Feeling the breeze hit my mane as I run round the grounds.
(I wouldn't want to carry anyone over with me.)
Instead sleeping longer and missing everyone.
Forgive me, if you will,
and there isn't any good explanation,
except I heard
deep in the inner soft
speaking of my ear,
that quiet space
to listen to the tongue.

A Wise Brown Moth

Here is my realization:
There are not one or two wise thoughts
but rather catching them on the fly
is possible but unlikely!

My days of wise thinking
may be no longer but perhaps that,
in fact, will make me wise!
This may be the grim wisdom of my heart.

The lighter wisdom floats on clouds like butterfly wings.
Just today, it flew as I walked along the very busy road,
on the grassy edge instead of the sidewalk:
a lovely moth flew low and I barely saw her.
And even more magically, she landed on the grass,
turning herself into a brown dried leaf:
which I watched as it walked!

Totem

Today the owl was near again. I was unable to see him, but his
presence was with me. I have a photo of him taken several
years ago when he first came to our home and remained for
hours, nearby outside. I stayed there too,
taking about 50 photos.
He is silent, mostly, like I am. He has wisdom, it seems.

I am thinking too much of late.
Hurting my brain with deep, complex thoughts!
Talking with my husband has given me insights about myself,
as well as my husband's mind, and the world at large!!
Perhaps my Beloved is like the wise owl, too!

Anyway, Bard Owl, you are my totem animal.
I hope you will not mind. I mean no harm to come to you.
Rather, I hold you in high esteem!

Upon computing an impossibility that there is anything but
Grace, I look out past the first visible trees, on into the deeper
woods, looking for the Wise Owl, and find him in
the silence there…

He brought Grace to my heart many years ago
and that same spot is now ringing with his song!

Musings

So if my spirit never dies,
does it follow on that I will live forever?
Plus, I promise my husband that
I will continue to talk to him long
after he has lost his mind...
But of course this house is too big for one person,
so please don't ever leave me here alone!

I never wake up thinking that
the spirit is not interested anymore.
Or that the spirit would give up.
Maybe I am just too much of an optimist
to believe in my own spirit ever giving up!
Maybe that is true for many of my friends, too!

Dissatisfied?

Still water.
So much of the time I claim myself as dissatisfied,
and then I look for a moment of stillness as a reward
if only I recognize it as such

Alzheimer's Love

My father lay on the couch
in the next room.
I could see him through the mesh
of the double-sided fireplace
as if we are neither caged
but something in between us is.
It is not the past,
and not the future,
but the present
that lies in a cage of uncertainty
but just as a pilot light remains true,
so do our hearts,
his while his mind struggles
to maintain itself in some dignity
of human questioning and effort,
mine flurrying against denial,
rage, and sorrow,
fully knowing ahead
is more fear and pain.

Yet we won't turn back now,
--perhaps there is no such choice--

but, yet, we *are* drawn forward
into that uncertain future by

the pull of warmth from
the flames of love.

We Are More Capable Than

We ever imagined.
The silence is draining.
We can go away and still be here!

In Search of the Brave Enough Prince

Lost count of them
Princes who came into my life
ready to slay dragons
but not quite up to it,
after all.

After each ending
I'd swear them off,
the lot of the gender
with an encompassing sweep
of my defeated hand.

I had wanted my hand
to hold his hand,
to walk on the path together
climbing hills in the way
crossing deep water safely,
one helping the other
each time it was needed.

I admit my lofty desire:
Heroism was what I wanted, and
Courage in the face of fear,
Hope in the time of discouragement,
Love in the battle of trials
when all is unknown.

I grew to mistrust words
or the intention behind words
until action backed it all up.
Love? Each declared love
but too soon, each time too soon.

For it was inevitable
I'd fall from the pedestal
of pretty, vulnerable damsel
and be the one I truly am,
the one I've always been.

I'm me, the Heroine
of all my tales.
For after each Prince
takes his leave,
this tarnished Princess
carries on,
wondering just a little
if the next Prince
will be the One.

Love...

doesn't live in a house.[6]

It stays in the heart

that is open

it laughs

with joy

in the heart

that is healthy

it cries if it must

in the heart

that is hurting.

The tears are

for healing,

ointment

that leaves a scar

that is somehow

much stronger

than before.

is in my heart.

Yet, I still want to

share a house

with you,

share the days and nights

with you.

I was already thinking

about dinner invitations

and my heart was feeling

giddy with joy

that I wanted to keep sharing

with others around me

especially you.

I can't stop loving you now.

Even still, I am sad about

your fears and want for you

to not feel that way.

118

Learning is like that.

Love is like that,

powerful and strong,

but also about joy,

and also about

human frailty.

That's how I feel

about you.

I

Love You

Very Much.

and for me

to not feel this way:

Afraid of the future,

sad about the past,

wondering about the moment.

I have to go on today,

make a cake,

prepare birthday for my son.

I

Must

Still Go On.

Notes

[1] Page 24. From *The Sanscrit.*

[2] Page 26. Sleeping Bear Dunes is a National Park along Lake Michigan on the north side of western Michigan. Dunes are unique and a fragile natural element in our world.

[3] Page 33. After a poem by Peter Cooley, using *Out of my darkness* as my prompt, starter.

[4] Page 73. This line by poet Caroline Forché prompted me to write a poem for my maternal grandmother during her final days. And my answer to the title question is always: Yes!

[5] Page 106. Many thanks to Lila Weisberger who found this poem in files she had kept while she was training me as a poetry therapist.

[6] Pages118-119. This poem is written in two voices, sharing one title. Please read each one in its entirety.

Made in the USA
Coppell, TX
25 March 2021

52339831R00080